The Leadership Handbook – A Primer on Leadership - The Greatest Authors & Books on Leadership

By George Mentz

All Rights Reserved 2020 Disclaimer for Mentzinger Media LLC

All works original herein except for writings from government websites in the public domain. Please consult a licensed professional before making any important decision.

First published by
Mentzinger Media, LTD

http://www.gmentz.com
Endorsed by the Academy http://www.gafm.com

© George Mentz 2020
The right of George Mentz to be identified as the author of this work has been asserted in accordance with the Copyright, Designs and Patents Act 1988.
ISBN – Disclosed on Publishing
ISBN - Disclosed on Publishing

Library of Congress Cataloguing-in-Publication Data
Cataloguing in Publication Data

A catalogue record for this book is available online

All rights reserved. No part of this manuscript or publication may be illegally copied, reproduced, stored in a retrieval system, or transmitted - in any form or by any means, electronic, mechanical, photocopying, recording and/or otherwise without the prior written express permission of the authors and or publishers. This book may not be lent, resold, scanned, hired out or otherwise disposed of by way of trade in any form, binding or cover other than that in which it is published, without the prior consent of the publishers.

Printed in the USA from Mentzinger Media, LLC USA

All insights or content in this document is information of a general nature and does not address the circumstances of any particular family, individual or entity. Nothing in the Site constitutes professional advice, medical advice, or financial advice. Please consult a licensed professional before making any important decision.

If you disagree with these Terms or are dissatisfied with this book or the author or the publication or publishing company, your sole and exclusive remedy is to discontinue using this book and its contents.

What is Leadership?

Leadership is both a skill and research area which includes the abilities of a person, team, department, or entity to lead or rather influence, inspire, or guide other individuals, groups or organizations.

U.S. academic environments define leadership as "a process of social influence in which a person can enlist the aid and support of others in the accomplishment of a common task".

Leadership research has produced concepts and strategies of leadership: involving traits, situational interaction, function, mental ability, behavior, power, vision and values, enthusiasm, focus, charisma, and intelligence, among others.

Below are some of the greatest books on leadership in history. From the Art of War by Sun Tzu to Stephen Covey, John Maxwell, Donald Trump and Rudy Giuliani, this book covers a quick VIP analysis of the greatest leadership books in history.

Table of Contents

What is Leadership? 3
History and Types of Leadership 5
Principles of Leadership in the Armed Forces. 6
    Create shared understanding 7
    Provide a clear organizational intent 7
    Exercise disciplined initiative 7
    Use mission orders 7
    Accept prudent risk 7
Ethics, Attributes and Virtues of Leadership 7
THE ART OF WAR 9
    Sun Tzu 9
HOW TO WIN FRIENDS AND INFLUENCE PEOPLE 11
    Dale Carnegie 11
On Becoming a Leader 12

Warren Bennis 12

First, Break All the Rules: What the World's Greatest Managers Do Differently 15

    Marcus Buckingham 15

Execution: The Discipline of Getting Things Done 17

    Larry Bossidy & Ram Charan 17

The One Minute Manager by Ken Blanchard 19

    Ken Blanchard & Spencer Johnson 19

Wooden on Leadership 20

    John Wooden & Steve Jamison 21

The Five Dysfunctions of a Team: A Leadership 22

    Patrick Lencioni 22

Good to Great: Why Some Companies Make the Leap ... and Others Don't 25

    Jim Collins 25

The Seven Habits of Highly Effective People 27

    Dr. Stephen Covey 27

The Innovator's Dilemma: When New Technologies Cause Great Firms to Fail 28

    Clayton Christensen 28

Leadership – By Giuliani 30

    Rudy Giuliani 30

Extreme Ownership: How U.S. Navy SEALs Lead and Win (12 Principles) 32

    Jocko Will ink and Leif Babine 32

The Lean Startup: How Today's Entrepreneurs Use Continuous Innovation to Create Radically Successful Businesses 34

    Eric Rise 34

The 21 Irrefutable Laws of Leadership: Follow Them and People Will Follow You 36

    John C. Maxwell 36

Leadership – By: Brian Tracy 38

    Brian Tracy 38

Principles: Life and Work 40

Ray Dalio 40

Lead Like Jesus Revisited: Lessons from the Greatest Leadership Role Model of All Time 42

Ken Blanchard and Phil Hodges 42

General Patton's Principles for Life and Leadership, 5th Edition 44

Porter B Williamson 44

Dare to Lead: Brave Work. Tough Conversations 46

Brené Brown 46

Outliers: The Story of Success 48

Malcolm Gladwell 48

Tools of Titans: The Tactics, Routines, and Habits 50

Tim Ferriss 50

The Millionaire Next Door: The Surprising Secrets 52

Thomas J. Stanley 52

Trump 101: The Way to Success 54

Donald J. Trump 54

Limitless: Upgrade Your Brain, Learn Anything Faster, and Unlock Your Exceptional Life Hardcover 55

Jim Kwik (Author) 55

Appendix – The Leadership and Consciousness Grid by Mentz 57

Author Biography – George Mentz, Esq. 63

History and Types of Leadership

Historically, some people argued that great leaders were born, not made. However, most people know that a person can be trained from childhood to have superior skills in many areas. Other traits may influence someone's leadership potential such as intelligence, assertiveness, physical ability or attractiveness.

Here are other attributes which affect people's leadership ability and success:

• Desire	• Learning ability
• Determination	• Focus
• Clarity	• Skills cultivation
• Enthusiasm	• Emotional mindset
• Initiative	• Communication ability
• Energy	• Adaptability
• Assertiveness	• Ability to teach
• Perseverance	• Skills
• Dominance	• Likeability

While there are various types of leadership, we must also look at the nature of a leader. Leaders can work as individuals, within a team, part of a group or even as a freelance leader in this new environment of the 21st century. Further, there is a clear difference between creative leadership and competitive leadership. A creative leader would be somebody who formulates something to solve problems where the solution helps people with health, wealth and prosperity. Competitive leadership is more focused on team or entity competition. Naturally, a leader in a team or company would be competing directly to out due or overcome a competitor whether it is football or international business competition.

While it is easy to wax philosophical about what leadership is, the 20+ book summaries and analysis below are packed with ideas about Leadership over the last 2,500 years. Below also is a brief outline of military leadership attributes which are included because the military is the originator of mission and project management which is part of every success.

Principles of Leadership in the Armed Forces.

Build cohesive teams through mutual trust
- Develops others—builds effective teams.
- Builds trust—sets personal example; sustains a climate of trust.
- Demonstrates the Organizational Values and decisions consistent with the Entity Ethic.
- Leads others—balances subordinate needs with mission requirements.
- Extends influence beyond the chain of command—builds consensus and resolves conflict.
- Creates a positive environment—fosters teamwork.

Create shared understanding
- Communicates—creates shared understanding.
- Demonstrates interpersonal tact—interaction with others.
- Leads others—provides purpose, motivation, and inspiration.
- Extends influence beyond the chain of command—uses understanding in diplomacy, negotiation, consensus building.
- Builds trust—uses appropriate methods of influence to energize others.
- Creates positive environment--supports learning.
- Gets results—designates, clarifies and deconflicts roles.

Provide a clear organizational intent
- Leads others—provides purpose.
- Communicates—employs engaging communication techniques.
- Gets results—prioritizes taskings.

Exercise disciplined initiative
- Leads others—influence others to take initiative.
- Demonstrates the Organizational Values—duty.
- Demonstrates self-discipline—maintains professional bearing and conduct.
- Demonstrates mental agility—anticipates uncertain or changing conditions.
- Gets results—accounts for commitment to task.

Use mission orders
- Leads others—provides purpose without excessive, detailed direction.
- Develops others—expands knowledge.
- Gets results—executes plans to accomplish the mission the right way.

Accept prudent risk
- Leads others—assesses and manages risk.
- Gets results—identifies, allocates, and manages resource

Citation: https://armypubs.army.mil/epubs/DR_pubs/DR_a/pdf/web/fm6_22.pdf

Ethics, Attributes and Virtues of Leadership
Here is a list of 33 Attributes of Leaders Compiled by Prof. Mentz

1. Right Senses – Sight, Feeling, Taste, Sound, Smell
2. Right Courtesy and Treatment of Others
3. Right Speech, Restraint of Tounge, and Brevity
4. Right Humility
5. Right Understanding -   Acute Listening
6. Right Attention and Right Witted
7. Right Moderation - Balance
8. Right Poise
9. Right Courage
10. Right Education & Righteous Self Reliance – Making the best of the self
11. Right Self Care– Rest - Avoidance of Gluttony
12. Right Zeal – Optimism
13. Right Tranquility (Peace of Mind)
14. Right Character
15. Right Preparation
16. Right Relations
17. Right Warriorship – Having the proper strength and self defense.
18. Right Giving and Generosity
19. Right Trust and Fidelity
20. Right Fellowship & Camaraderie
21. Right Purpose – Authenticity and Usefulness
22. Right Perception and Wisdom
23. Right Action
24. Right Dignity and Integrity
25. Right Gratitude and Thankfulness - Praise
26. Right Aliveness – You are engaged in Living Actively
27. Right Prosperity – Righteous creation and use of Wealth
28. Right Legacy - Right Offspring & Integrity
29. Right Effort
30. Right Meditation and Contemplation
31. Right Love and Respect
32. Right Thinking
33. Right Karma – Creating great consequences thought action and deeds.

BOOK TITLE	THE ART OF WAR
AUTHOR	Sun Tzu
PUBLISHED	Oxford University press (1963)

BEST QUOTES OR INSIGHTS

"The greatest victory is that which requires no battle"

"Victorious warriors win first and then go to war, while defeated warriors go to war first and then seek to win"

"If you know the enemy and you know yourself, you need not fear the result of a hundred battles. If you know yourself but not the enemy, for every victory gained you will also suffer a defeat. If you know neither the enemy nor yourself, you will succumb in every battle"

"Who wishes to fight must first count the cost"

SUMMARY THEME OF BOOK

The foremost critical point of the art of war is that the information is much incumbent and an educated guess is far better than a gut decision carried by an individual. Further in the story the sun Tzu conclude the generals should consider the "military calculus" of examining everything that could have an impact on the result of a battle.

KEY TAKEAWAYS OR BEST TIPS

- "Victorious warriors win first and then go to war, while defeated warriors go to war first and then seek to win"
- Use your personal energy and charisma to help yourself and team, but also allow your team to assist you in any way that will allow your team be a unified to assist people with risk and opportunity.
- Be prepared to respond to shifting circumstances successfully.
- Know your people, team, or customers. Communicate with them the information they need to make informed decisions or utilize the benefits that you offer.
- Competitive intelligence and benchmarking allow you to know your competition, know your customer, and know your target.

SUCCESS ANALYSIS – ART OF WAR

Furthermore, the book also possess a detailed definition and elaboration of the weapons the Chinese military own. Besides, the Chinese strategy including the rank to discipline, is elaborated. The sun also stressed the incumbency of the intelligence operatives and the war efforts. Since the sun was much renowned for his military tactics and his teachings also including his analytical strategies, his strategy and ideas primarily formed the basis of the military training of higher level for advanced levels for almost a millennium.

MORE INFO	https://www.ancient.eu/Sun-Tzu/		
Other books			

BOOK TITLE	HOW TO WIN FRIENDS AND INFLUENCE PEOPLE
AUTHOR	Dale Carnegie
PUBLISHED	Simon and Schuster (1936)

BEST QUOTES OR INSIGHTS

> "It isn't what you have or who you are or where you are or what you are doing that makes you happy or unhappy. It is what you think about it."

> "Don't be afraid of enemies who attack you. Be afraid of the friends who flatter you."

> "Develop success from failures. Discouragement and failure are two of the surest stepping stones to success."

SUMMARY THEME OF BOOK

The book commits the fact that one should not criticize or complain. The primary idea of this that a person could easily change bring up a change in other people behavior by only changing his behavior. It primarily teaches a person the ethics and principles of understanding other people better and to become a likeable person who is usually considered more and have much improved relations through only key aspect of leadership. Criticism is dangerous. It further tends to place an individual on the defensive part which will condemn him to justify himself. It further wounds a person's pride, destroys his sense of importance and also introduces resentment.

KEY TAKEAWAYS OR BEST TIPS

- "When dealing with people, remember you are not dealing with creatures of logic, but with creatures bristling with prejudice and motivated by pride and vanity."
- Become sincerely interested in other people and their lives.
- Learn to Smile.
- Remember a person's name as it is the sweetest sound to others in any language.
- The book is designed to: Get you out of a mental rut, give you new thoughts, new visions, new ambitions, enable you to make friends quickly and easily, and increase your popularity.

SUCCESS ANALYSIS – HOW TO WIN FRIENDS			
people often tend to learn more knowledge and also enhance their learning speed if they are treated with good behavior rather than bad behavior. Through criticizing people don't tend to make an effective option but cause resentment. Flattery is much selfish act and insecure. It also a cheap praise that a person is told what he thinks about himself. In the longer run the flattery tends to do much harm than good.			
MORE INFO	https://www.dalecarnegie.com/		
Other books			

BOOK TITLE	On Becoming a Leader
AUTHOR	Warren Bennis
PUBLISHED	Reading, MA: Addison-Wesley (1989).

BEST QUOTES OR INSIGHTS

"If knowing yourself and being yourself were as easy to do as to talk about, there wouldn't be nearly so many people walking around in borrowed postures, spouting secondhand ideas, trying desperately to fit in rather than to stand out."

"...once you recognize, or admit, that your primary goal is to fully express yourself, you will find the means to achieve the rest of your goals..."

"The opposite of hope is despair, and when we despair, it is because we feel there are no choices."

SUMMARY THEME OF BOOK

In the mid of 1980s, the Warren Bennis further wrote this type of classic model leadership which is based on the personal growth, self-expression, integrity and learning, drawing from interviews with dozens of leaders. Further, he also identified that leaders do not usually tend to find lead. But they tend to express themselves in best manner

KEY TAKEAWAYS OR BEST TIPS

- "In a time of drastic change, it is the learners who inherit the future. The learned find themselves equipped to live in a world that no longer exists."

- Becoming a leader has many attributes: Continuous education and never-ending curiosity

- Having a compelling vision; leaders first define their objectives and then set about managing their destiny.

SUCCESS ANALYSIS – ON BECOMING A LEADER			
Furthermore, an individual must not agree with the Bennis decisions of the role models, and also his recurring innuendos may try to misplace the readers who have difference in their alignment, but this wouldn't keep any from reading book. The primary difference between this text and leaders is that the effective leadership is described by the leaders, whereas while the person becomes a leader, he tends to give guidance about becoming an effective leader. Like the leaders tend to talk about the significance of communication.			
MORE INFO	https://www.google.com/url?sa=t&rct=j&q=&esrc=s&source=web&cd=&ved=2ahUKEwj8k534jYXtAhVyt3EKHdOPDh4QFjAJegQIKRAC&url=https%3A%2F%2Fwww.basicbooks.com%2Ftitles%2Fwarren-g-bennis%2Fon-becoming-a-leader%2F9780465014088%2F&usg=AOvVaw1ebnSVFbgS1vmELASFSjkK		
Other books			

BOOK TITLE	
	First, Break All the Rules: What the World's Greatest Managers Do Differently
AUTHOR	Marcus Buckingham
PUBLISHED	May 1999 (Simon & Schuster)

BEST QUOTES OR INSIGHTS

"Talent is the multiplier. The more energy and attention you invest in it, the greater the yield. The time you spend with your best is, quite simply, your most productive time."

"People leave managers, not companies"

"People don't change that much. Instead of trying to put in what God left out, try drawing out what God left in!"

SUMMARY THEME OF BOOK

The Gallup's research is based on the 80000 managers and 400 companies which process twelve different questions which differentiate the powerful departments. First, break all rules which introduces the significant measuring stick and highlights the employee opinion and productivity, customer satisfaction and the ray of turnover

KEY TAKEAWAYS OR BEST TIPS

- "The talented employee may join a company because of its charismatic leaders, its generous benefits, and its world-class training programs, but how long that employee stays and how productive he is while he is there is determined by his relationship with his immediate supervisor."

- This book shows how top managers pick an employee for their talents rather than for degrees or experience. Then leaders set expectations and help build on each person's abilities rather than focusing on limitations to get the highest performance within a group, individual or organization.

SUCCESS ANALYSIS – FIRST BREAK ALL THE RULES

The companies also compete to search for best employees and hire them using benefits, pay, promotions and training. But these well intention efforts often tend to miss the mark. The attraction for talented managers is the front-line manager. The amazing book further elaborates how the best manager could select the employees for talent instead of skills. Thus, this also includes the training about how to set the expectations, how they inspire individual and how they enhance the abilities.

MORE INFO	https://www.google.com/url?sa=t&rct=j&q=&esrc=s&source=web&cd=&ved=2ahUKEwiJtLfaj4XtAhVaSxUIHbkJAYcQFjAEegQIBxAC&url=https%3A%2F%2Fwww.businessinsider.com%2Flessons-from-first-break-all-the-rules-2016-9&usg=AOvVaw06n4zOBSjcKqehRWr0te9-.		
Other books			

BOOK TITLE	Execution: The Discipline of Getting Things Done
AUTHOR	Larry Bossidy & Ram Charan
PUBLISHED	Random House, 2011.

BEST QUOTES OR INSIGHTS

"But if you have to choose between someone with a staggering IQ and an elite education who's gliding along, and someone with a lower IQ but who is absolutely determined to succeed, you'll always do better with the second person."

"The foundation of changing behavior is linking rewards to performance and making the linkages transparent."

"The hardware of a computer is useless without the right software. Similarly, in an organization the hardware (strategy and structure) is inert without the software (beliefs and behaviors)."

SUMMARY THEME OF BOOK

Execution: The Discipline of Getting Things Done by Lawrence Bossidy and Ram Charan is a 3-part assessment on what the companies require to fully succeed through various strategies, process, leadership and the execution. Thus, through this the companies become successful rather than failing. It is much incumbent for the business leaders to be aware about how to execute in a best manner. The execution is the main process. Every time asking about how and what questions are still accountable.

KEY TAKEAWAYS OR BEST TIPS

"The leader must be in charge of getting things done by running the three core processes—picking other leaders, setting the strategic direction, and conducting operations."

The book analyzes what it takes to succeed through strategies, processes, leadership and ultimately, the action of execution.

SUCCESS ANALYSIS - EXECUTIION

The part of the execution means that a person is required to be in the position to be understood I'm the business environment and the organizing capabilities. The business leaders have three most important roles when it moves towards the execution. The selection of the right people, the strategic directions and the operations of coordination are required.

MORE INFO			
Other books			

BOOK TITLE	The One Minute Manager by Ken Blanchard
AUTHOR	Ken Blanchard & Spencer Johnson
PUBLISHED	*Quarterly* 23.4 (1983): 39-41.

BEST QUOTES OR INSIGHTS

- *The key to successful leadership today is influence, not authority.*
- *Feedback is the breakfast of champions.*
- *None of us is as smart as all of us.*
- *"Take a minute: look at your goals, look at your performance, see if your behavior matches your goals."*

SUMMARY THEME OF BOOK

The one minute manager produces three simple tools for the managers, which each utilizes almost 60 seconds or much lesser, but can assist to improve how to do their job. It also includes the motivation and the great works which are ought to be delivered happily. The idea behind the principle is mainly the fact that the people who tends to feel good will also deliver good outcomes. When the one minutes catches a person to something good, he praises the person by explaining what he tends to see and how it impacts his mood.

KEY TAKEAWAYS OR BEST TIPS

- "Victorious warriors win first and then go to war, while defeated warriors go to war first and then seek to win.
- For a manager to be perceived as a positive manager, they need a four to one positive to negative contact ratio.
- In the past a leader was a boss. Today's leaders must be partners with their people... they no longer can lead solely based on positional power.

SUCCESS ANALYSIS – ONE MINUTE MANAGER			
<ul><li>Agree on Written goals (no more than half a dozen) with staff members.</li><li>Staff should re-read the goals and document progress</li><li>Rebuke non-productive action or behaviour, and remind the person how much they are valued.</li></ul>			
MORE INFO	https://journals.sagepub.com/doi/abs/10.1177/001088048302300409		
Other books			

BOOK TITLE	
	Wooden on Leadership

AUTHOR	John Wooden & Steve Jamison
PUBLISHED	McGraw Hill, 2005

BEST QUOTES OR INSIGHTS

"Good values are like a magnet – they attract good people." "Who you are inside – what you believe – is important, but what you do means more, much more."

"Before telling someone what to do you must teach him how to do it." "Emotionalism destroys consistency".

SUMMARY THEME OF BOOK

Legendary basketball coach John Wooden put together an excellent book on leadership and character.

KEY TAKEAWAYS:

1. Focus on "the tasks" and success will follow
2. Practice calm intensity on the task at hand
3. How you do small things is how you do everything
4. Prioritize the team success over the individual
5. Suggest, don't be too BOSSY

KEY TAKEAWAYS OR BEST TIPS

"Good values are like a magnet – they attract good people." "Who you are inside – what you believe – is important, but what you do means more, much more."

SUCCESS ANALYSIS – WOODEN ON LEADERSHIP

Further, the straightforward method posses the winning shots, athletic metaphor, game time prep talks personal and private experiences and other situations. The real fire tend to happen behind the scenes, the minor and larger mind games and the jnner battles. The authors dont intemd to impose a thepry which is related to sports with some principles and syrategies. Thus, this book is much recomended to every sport oriented people, the stregjstst, the mangets and the oridnary people who are keen to leave a mark om this land.

MORE INFO	Click here to enter Link.		
Other books			

BOOK TITLE	
	The Five Dysfunctions of a Team: A Leadership

AUTHOR	Patrick Lencioni
PUBLISHED	*Pfeiffer, a Wiley Imprint.* 2012.

BEST QUOTES OR INSIGHTS

"Trust is knowing that when a team member does push you, they're doing it because they care about the team."

"Remember teamwork begins by building trust. And the only way to do that is to overcome our need for invulnerability."

"Great teams do not hold back with one another. They are unafraid to air their dirty laundry. They admit their mistakes, their weaknesses, and their concerns without fear of reprisal."

"Politics is when people choose their words and actions based on how they want others to react rather than based on what they really think."

SUMMARY THEME OF BOOK

According to the book, the five type of dysfunctions are: the absence of the trust- reluctant to the group. The fear of conflict- the search for the artificial harmony over debate. However, the absence of commitment creates ambiguity in the organization.

KEY TAKEAWAYS OR BEST TIPS

"It's as simple as this. When people don't unload their opinions and feel like they've been listened to, they won't really get on board."

DYSFUNCTION #1: ABSENCE OF TRUST. Role of the leader: Encourage the building of trust on a team by demonstrating vulnerability first.

DYSFUNCTION #2: FEAR OF CONFLICT. ...

DYSFUNCTION #3: LACK OF COMMITMENT. ...

DYSFUNCTION #4: AVOIDANCE OF ACCOUNTABILITY. ...

DYSFUNCTION #5: INATTENTION TO RESULTS.

SUCCESS ANALYSIS – FIVE DYSFUNCTIONS

This book explores the fundamental causes of failure in organizations and teams. Like some of Lencioni's other books, the bulk of it is written as a story or fable.			
MORE INFO	https://www.tablegroup.com/books/dysfunctions/		
Other books			

BOOK TITLE	Good to Great: Why Some Companies Make the Leap ... and Others Don't
AUTHOR	Jim Collins
PUBLISHED	HarperCollins 2009

BEST QUOTES OR INSIGHTS

"The purpose of bureaucracy is to compensate for incompetence and lack of discipline."

"Greatness is not a function of circumstance. Greatness, it turns out, is largely a matter of conscious choice, and discipline."

"Great vision without great people is irrelevant."

"A company should limit its growth based on its ability to attract enough of the right people."

SUMMARY THEME OF BOOK

The idea that inspired this book was to answer questions about how good companies might become great companies, and how they went about the analysis.

KEY TAKEAWAYS OR BEST TIPS

The typical start-ups don't become great companies. As a small company grows, bureaucracy and rules make up for incompetence and lack of discipline. To avoid over-burdensome frameworks in business, instill a culture of discipline of people, thought and action.

- Disciplined people: means recruiting great people and keeping them focused on excellence.
- Disciplined thought: means communicating honestly about the facts while avoiding getting sidetracked.
- Disciplined action: means comprehending what is important and urgent to achieve and what is not.

SUCCESS ANALYSIS – GOOD TO GREAT

Level 5 leadership is a concept in the book Good to Great. Level 5 leaders have a powerful blend of: humility and willpower. Level 5 leaders are super ambitious, but their ambition is devoted to the organizational objectives and its purpose, and not just for themselves.

MORE INFO	https://www.jimcollins.com/		
Other books			

BOOK TITLE	
	The Seven Habits of Highly Effective People
AUTHOR	Dr. Stephen Covey
PUBLISHED	1989

BEST QUOTES OR INSIGHTS

Creating Win Win Deals is part of the 7 Habits - Genuinely strive for mutually beneficial solutions or agreements in your relationships. Value and respect people by understanding a "win" for all concerned is ultimately a better long-term resolution than if only one person in the situation had gotten his way.

SUMMARY THEME OF BOOK

The Seven Habits of Highly Effective People, first published in 1989, is a business and self-help book written by Stephen R. Covey. It has sold more than 25 million copies in 38 languages worldwide. The book discusses 7 timeless success tactics they Covey developed by studying the greatest self help figures in recent history.

KEY TAKEAWAYS OR BEST TIPS

Covey coined the idea of abundance mentality or abundance mindset, a concept in which a person believes there are enough resources and success to share with others. He contrasts it with the scarcity mindset. Also, **Habit 7 is about how to " Sharpen the Saw"** Sharpening the Saw is about maintaining: Balance and renewing your resources, energy, and health to create a sustainable, long-term, effective lifestyle. It primarily emphasizes exercise for physical renewal, prayer (meditation, yoga, etc.) and good study & reading for mental renewal. It also mentions service to society for spiritual renewal.

SUCCESS ANALYSIS

- Putting your life in perspective is a key part of the book's concepts. What would you want said at your own funeral? What would you want to have been, done, or had in you life?

MORE INFO	https://www.franklincovey.com/the-7-habits.html		

BOOK TITLE	The Innovator's Dilemma: When New Technologies Cause Great Firms to Fail
AUTHOR	Clayton Christensen
PUBLISHED	Harvard Business Review Press, 2013.

BEST QUOTES OR INSIGHTS

"Disruptive technologies typically enable new markets to emerge."

"Disruptive technology should be framed as a marketing challenge, not a technological one."

"To succeed consistently, good managers need to be skilled not just in choosing, training, and motivating the right people for the right job, but in choosing, building, and preparing the right organization for the job as well."

SUMMARY THEME OF BOOK

The organizational culture and the capability to innovate is the key terms that for relationship under the study of Innovator's dilemmas. New agile organizations tend to innovate much easier with the disruptive technology as they are not related with the outdated norms and values or organizational values.

KEY TAKEAWAYS OR BEST TIPS

"Disruptive technology should be framed as a marketing challenge, not a technological one."

The Innovator's Dilemma is a classic leadership book that explains the nature of disruption and why some market leaders fail as new technologies and industries change and what leadership can do to obtain market leadership with longevity.

SUCCESS ANALYSIS – INNOVATORS DILEMMA

Laws of Disruptive Technologies

1) Companies rely on customers & investors for resources.

2) Small markets don't meet the growth needs of large companies.

3) Markets that don't exist can't be analyzed.

4) An organization's capabilities define its weaknesses

5) Technologies can progress faster than the markets demand.

MORE INFO	Click here to enter Link.		
Other books			

BOOK TITLE	Leadership – By Giuliani
AUTHOR	Rudy Giuliani
PUBLISHED	Hyperion, 2002

BEST QUOTES OR INSIGHTS

"Change is not a destination, just as hope is not a strategy."

"My father used to say to me, 'Whenever you get into a jam, whenever you get into a crisis or an emergency…become the calmest person in the room and you'll be able to figure your way out of it."

"This is not a personal attack. It's a statement of fact - Barack Obama has never led anything."

"White police officers won't be there if you weren't killing each other 70 percent of the time"

SUMMARY THEME OF BOOK

Leadership (published October 1, 2002, ISBN 0-7868-6841-4) is a book written by Rudolph W. Giuliani (co-authored with Ken Kurson) about his time as the mayor of the city of New York and the way he reduced the crime, and also revitalized the economy of his city. Furthermore, much of the book was written before the September 11 year 2001 attacks, through Giuliani intended to possess a possess whole section of the way he dealt with the emergency and his various experiences.

In the year 2007, the book was tended to be re-issued in the Giuliani's presidential campaign, with a completely new introduction which also includes the significant respective significant respective significant respective significant the respective of Giulani about the various significamt problems facing the united states.

KEY TAKEAWAYS OR BEST TIPS

"To be locked into partisan politics doesn't permit you to think clearly."

Born in Brooklyn, New York, Rudolph W. Giuliani was elected mayor of New York City in 1993. He was The principles he espouses are: prioritize, prepare, take responsibility, hold everyone accountable, recruit great individuals, reflect, analyze, then decide, under-promise and over-deliver, develop and employ strong principles, and be loyal and purposeful.

SUCCESS ANALYSIS

The book further tends to highlight the change that gives the excellent foundation which could be easily applied in day to day situation.

- The problems of the area must be statistically analyses
- High level accountability
- "Broken Window" theory of policing (which is the primary theory of minor crimes to set a significant tome for major ones)
- A future constituted by a positive and vividly bright vision.

MORE INFO			
Other books			

BOOK TITLE	Extreme Ownership: How U.S. Navy SEALs Lead and Win (12 Principles)
AUTHOR	Jocko Will ink and Leif Babine
PUBLISHED	St. Martin's Press, 2017.

BEST QUOTES OR INSIGHTS

"The advantage of "Extreme Ownership" is that it generates dynamism. It pushes you to act and it is thus no longer possible to wallow in complaints and criticism."

SUMMARY THEME OF BOOK

The book explains the military terms and the regulations which the individuals have to face. The book develops the ideals which will help in the effective generation of the ideals of battle field for human growth and progression. The applications of the principles of leadership which are used by the military in the battlefields have been developed by the author in the business world in the book.

KEY TAKEAWAYS OR BEST TIPS

The emphasis is that responsibility exist for all stakeholders and individuals. They must be prepared to deal with the consequences of their decisions for the team and as an asset, and avoid blame.

1. Extreme Ownership - Take complete responsibility for all your results
2. There are no bad teams, only bad leaders
3. You have to believe if you want to win
4. Check your ego
5. Cover and Move - Ensure the team is clear on the mission.
6. Keep things simple
7. Leaders need to prioritize and execute.
8. Decentralized Command
9. Identify clear directives for the team
10. Lead up and down the chain of command
11. Decisiveness amid uncertainty
12. Discipline equals freedom

SUCCESS ANALYSIS			
The book explains the practice of extreme ownership. This type of ownership discusses the practice of owning everything present in this world. Thus, the ownership of the objective is taken to an extreme degree.			
MORE INFO			
Other books			

BOOK TITLE	
	The Lean Startup: How Today's Entrepreneurs Use Continuous Innovation to Create Radically Successful Businesses
AUTHOR	Eric Rise
PUBLISHED	Crown Business, 2011

BEST QUOTES OR INSIGHTS

"The only way to win is to learn faster than anyone else."

"We must learn what customers really want, not what they say they want or what we think they should want."

"Reading is good, action is better."

SUMMARY THEME OF BOOK

The book discusses the main ideology which is effective for the regulation of human systematic development and life progression. The main ideals begin the effective development of entrepreneur's shave been defined in this group study. Thus, it is important for the regulation of working and systematic working in business environments, it is a common issue which deals with the failure of entrepreneur. The book discusses effective stances which will help in the regulation of environment.

KEY TAKEAWAYS OR BEST TIPS

1. "As you consider building your own minimum viable product, let this simple rule suffice: remove any feature, process, or effort that does not contribute directly to the learning you seek."

2. Observe and Measure Customer Behavior

3. Be Comfortable Pivoting based on Key Information

4. Remain Lean and Agile

SUCCESS ANALYSIS – THE LEAN STARTUP

The book contained a detailed explanation and analysis of the past and current experiences of the writer in terms of the book. The development of an effective working environments has been effective for the development of individuals.

MORE INFO	http://theleanstartup.com/		
Other books			

BOOK TITLE	The 21 Irrefutable Laws of Leadership: Follow Them and People Will Follow You
AUTHOR	John C. Maxwell
PUBLISHED	HarperCollins Leadership, 2007.

BEST QUOTES OR INSIGHTS

"We cannot become what we need by remaining what we are."
"Change is inevitable. Growth is optional."

"The greatest day in your life and mine is when we take total "Leaders must be close enough to relate to others, but far enough ahead to motivate them. "responsibility for our attitudes. That's the day we truly grow up."

"Success is... knowing your purpose in life, growing to reach your maximum potential, and sowing seeds that benefit others."

SUMMARY THEME OF BOOK

The book reflects on the various laws which will help in the development of the individual working techniques and will allow the effective regulation of efforts which will lead towards success. The development of effectiveness and the ability to determine the effectiveness of an individual's is essentially based on the system of working and regulation. Following the law of influence will be effective for the development of character, relationships, knowledge and intuition in an individual. The cultivation of experience, past successes and ability will allow the effective innovation of the structure of the company.

KEY TAKEAWAYS OR BEST TIPS

"Seven Steps to Success
1) Make a commitment to grow daily.
2) Value the process more than events.
3) Don't wait for inspiration.
4) Be willing to sacrifice pleasure for opportunity.
5) Dream big.
6) Plan your priorities.
7) Give up to go up."

SUCCESS ANALYSIS – 21 IRREFUTABLE LAWS OF LEADERSHIP

The law of progress allows the investments of indviulas in a form which allows effective regulation of learning development and will help in the improvement of skills and development. The effective regulation of improvement of success and functioning will be helpful for the systematic working of company's; growth and regulation

MORE INFO	https://www.johnmaxwell.com/		
Other books			

BOOK TITLE	Leadership – By: Brian Tracy
AUTHOR	Brian Tracy
PUBLISHED	Jaico Publishing House, 2008.

BEST QUOTES OR INSIGHTS

- ""Integrity Is the Most Valuable and Respected Quality of Leadership. Always Keep Your Word."
- "Leadership Is the Ability to Get Extraordinary Achievement from Ordinary People"
- "Leaders Set High Standards. Refuse to Tolerate Mediocrity Or Poor Performance"
- "The Best Leaders Have A High Consideration Factor. They Really Care About Their People"

SUMMARY THEME OF BOOK

Tracy helps in the development of modern-day leaders. His book discusses the basics ideals which are required for the effective working of the system. The specification of goals has been essential for decisive function and effective motivation of an individuals. Tracy is an advocate of focusing on what is important in work and getting that productive work done before anything else.

KEY TAKEAWAYS OR BEST TIPS

- ""Clarity Is the Key To Effective Leadership. What Are Your Goals?"
- Tracy believes that we all have the ability to: Inspire trust in others, create confidence, and cultivate loyalty and bring a sense of meaning and purpose to your organization
- Tap into the energy and enthusiasm that compels people to commit to your vision.

SUCCESS ANALYSIS – LEADERSHIP – BRIAN TRACY

The book contained a detailed explanation and analysis of the management and leadership development skills which ranks from discipline to increased innovation in market. The author argues that the various dynamic timings require effective evaluation of challenges and opportunities. Thus, it is essential that the modern human life allows the development of the individual character to navigate the environment and business.

MORE INFO	https://www.briantracy.com/		
Other books			

BOOK TITLE	Principles: Life and Work
AUTHOR	Ray Dalio
PUBLISHED	Simon and Schuster, 2017.

BEST QUOTES OR INSIGHTS

"It is far more common for people to allow ego to stand in the way of learning."

"Above all else, I want you to think for yourself, to decide 1) what you want, 2) what is true and 3) what to do about it"

"Great is better than terrible, and terrible is better than mediocre, because terrible at least gives life flavor."

"What I wanted was to have an interesting, diverse life filled with lots of learning - and especially meaningful work and meaningful relationships. I feel that I have gotten these in abundance and I am happy."

SUMMARY THEME OF BOOK

The book discusses the effective and developed principles which will help in the regulation of the interpersonal management techniques. The generation of a unique and effective company culture is done in the book. Ray Dalio have developed an effective set of principles which have been equally and effectively beneficial for the development of human life and development of radical honesty and radical transparency system in a working environment. the development of productivity and the effective collective thinking have bene a source of development and individual life growth and development.

KEY TAKEAWAYS OR BEST TIPS

- "Pain + Reflection = Progress"
- The main theme is that finding truth is the most effective path to make decisions, and further: the ego, emotion, and blind spots inhibit you from discovering reality.

SUCCESS ANALYSIS – PRINCIPLES LIFE & WORK DALIO

The development of meritocracy and believability-weight in the development of human ideals have been termed as effective. Thus, for the continual improvement in a system, the effective working of a group is essential and more developmental.

Use the 5-Step Process to get what you want out of life which is based in the fundamentals of project management.

1. Have clear goals.
2. Identify the challenges that stand in your way.
3. Diagnose the problems and find their causes.
4. Create plans or solutions that will get you past the problems.
5. Do the actions necessary to achieve results.

MORE INFO	https://www.principles.com/		
Other books			

BOOK TITLE	Lead Like Jesus Revisited: Lessons from the Greatest Leadership Role Model of All Time
AUTHOR	Ken Blanchard and Phil Hodges
PUBLISHED	Thomas Nelson, 2016

BEST QUOTES OR INSIGHTS

- "Self-promotion (pride) and self-protection (fear) dominate today's leadership style. Many leaders act as if the sheep are there only for the benefit of the shepherd."
- "This alternative approach to leadership is driven by four basic beliefs that have become central to our ministry: • Leadership happens anytime we influence the thinking, behavior, or development of another person. • Jesus is the greatest leadership role model of all time. Servant leadership is the only approach to leadership that Jesus validates for His followers. • Effective leadership begins on the inside, with our hearts"
- "For followers of Jesus, servant leadership is not an option; servant leadership is a mandate"

SUMMARY THEME OF BOOK

Four areas of leadership in the book are

- Heart - What is the primary motivation for you as a leader, whether as head of a family, church, or a large corporation?

- Head - What are your core beliefs and viewpoints about leadership?

- Hands - Do you set specific goals and measure performance, consistently monitoring and communicating with those you lead?

- Habits — How do you refresh and revitalize yourself as a leader?

KEY TAKEAWAYS OR BEST TIPS

"Leading like Jesus is a transformational journey. This transformational journey begins with the willingness to do whatever Jesus commands, with a heart surrendered to doing His will, and with the commitment to lead the way He leads".

"Leading like Jesus requires leaders to be shepherds and servants, who value each person as an integral part of the organization".

A goal is a specific event that, once achieved, becomes a piece of history to be superseded by a new goal. A vision, or view of the future, is an ongoing, evolving, hopeful look into the future that stirs the hearts and minds of people who know they will never see its end or limit.

3 The Head Of A Servant Leader, Page 88

SUCCESS ANALYSIS – LEAD LIKE JESUS

The authors guide readers through the process of evaluating how to lead like Jesus. Blanchard describes process of aligning two internal domains—the heart and the head—and two external domains—the hands and the habits.

MORE INFO	https://www.kenblanchardbooks.com		
Other books			

BOOK TITLE	General Patton's Principles for Life and Leadership, 5th Edition
AUTHOR	Porter B Williamson
PUBLISHED	Management and Systems Consultants, 1988.

BEST QUOTES OR INSIGHTS

- "Though I may walk through the valley of the shadow of death, I will never fear no evil, for I am the meanest mother ****er in the valley"
- "politicians are the lowest forms of life on earth. democrats are the lowest forms of politicians"
- "a leader is a man who can adapt principles to circumstances"

SUMMARY THEME OF BOOK

Patton's principles of command and management:

- Say what you mean and mean what you say.
- Always be alert to the source of problems.
- Select leaders for success and not from emotion or affection.
- Leaders must have the authority to match his responsibility.

KEY TAKEAWAYS OR BEST TIPS

- "The object of war is not to die for your country but to make the other bastard die for his"
- Say what you mean and mean what you say. Always be alert to the source of trouble. Select leaders for accomplishment and not for affection. Every leader must have the authority to match his responsibility.

SUCCESS ANALYSIS – PATTON ON LIFE AND LEADERSHIP

The book discusses the attributes associated with Leadership and an effective command. The book uses various interviews from soldiers which exemplify General's patterns and working system and his daily attributes of working. The physical Fitness, Pride-Courage-Confidence, Decisions, Success, and Life & Death are discussed in the book.

Patton's principles for decision making:

1. It is our deeds and not we do not say that will destroy us.
2. Communication with the staffs and troops.
3. Know what you know and understand what you do NOT know.
4. Never make decisions too early or too late.

MORE INFO			
Other books			

BOOK TITLE	Dare to Lead: Brave Work. Tough Conversations
AUTHOR	Brené Brown
PUBLISHED	Random House 2018

BEST QUOTES OR INSIGHTS

"At the end of the day, at the end of the week, at the end of my life, I want to say I contributed more than I criticized"

"I define a leader as anyone who takes responsibility for finding the potential in people and processes, and who has the courage to develop that potential"

"The courage to be vulnerable is not about winning or losing, it's about the courage to show up when you can't predict or control the outcome"

"People are opting out of vital conversations about diversity and inclusivity because they fear looking wrong, saying something wrong, or being wrong. Choosing our own comfort over hard conversations is the epitome of privilege, and it corrodes trust and moves us away from meaningful and lasting change."

SUMMARY THEME OF BOOK

Dare To Lead - dispels common myths about the 21st century culture and shows us that authentic leadership requires: vulnerability, values, trust, and resilience.

KEY TAKEAWAYS OR BEST TIPS

- "We fail the minute we let someone else define success for us"
- Daring leadership is a mosaic of four skills that are teachable, observable, and measurable: Rumbling with Vulnerability, Living into our Values, Braving Trust, and Learning to Rise.

SUCCESS ANALYSIS – DARE TO LEAD

#1 – We need to have the tough conversations. First, with our inner self. Then, with your group. You cannot, you must not, avoid the important communications!

#2 – Identify your core principles; and then, engage your principles. Practice them! Live them!

#3 – Aim for mastery. Progress not just perfection. Learn to give and receive feedback.

#4 – Breathe. Practice taking breaths. (Count to four: inhale by nose; hold; exhale by your mouth).

#5 – Give careful attention to the stories you tell in mind or vocally – to and about yourself; to others ; and your company; and our world.

#6 – Be courageous enough to be vulnerable. This opens your life to growth and mastery.

MORE INFO			
Other books			

BOOK TITLE	Outliers: The Story of Success
AUTHOR	Malcolm Gladwell
PUBLISHED	Little, Brown and company 2008.

BEST QUOTES OR INSIGHTS

"Practice isn't the thing you do once you're good. It's the thing you do that makes you good"

"Who we are cannot be separated from where we're from"

"Those three things - autonomy, complexity, and a connection between effort and reward - are, most people will agree, the three qualities that work has to have if it is to be satisfying."

"if you work hard enough and assert yourself, and use your mind and imagination, you can shape the world to your desires. (151)"

SUMMARY THEME OF BOOK

Success is about more than just innate ability. Success is combined with various key factors such as opportunities, meaningful hard work, and your cultural legacy. Random factors can influence the creativity and opportunities you have.

KEY TAKEAWAYS OR BEST TIPS

"It is those who are successful, in other words, who are most likely to be given the kinds of special opportunities that lead to further success. It's the rich who get the biggest tax breaks. It's the best students who get the best teaching and most attention. And it's the biggest nine- and ten-year-olds who get the most coaching and practice. However, a child without a video game may actually become the best at reading, math, science, and writing or other creative opportunities. Success is the result of what sociologists like to call "accumulative advantage".

SUCCESS ANALYSIS - OUTLIERS

Malcolm Gladwell's biggest objective in Outliers is to analyze achievement and failure as cultural phenomena and variables in order to determine the factors that typically influence or foster success.

MORE INFO	https://www.gladwellbooks.com/		
Other books			

BOOK TITLE	Tools of Titans: The Tactics, Routines, and Habits
AUTHOR	Tim Ferriss
PUBLISHED	Houghton Mifflin, 2017.

BEST QUOTES OR INSIGHTS

""The world is changed by your example, not by your opinion."

"Productivity is for robots. What humans are going to be really good at is asking questions, being creative, and experiences."

"The most important trick to be happy is to realize that happiness is a choice that you make and a skill that you develop. You choose to be happy, and then you work at it. It's just like building muscles"

"Losers have goals. Winners have systems"

SUMMARY THEME OF BOOK

The book is massive compendium, which deals with everything which the author has learnt regarding the development of health, wealth and wisdom in life. Ferriss gathered the data from: interviewing over 200 world-class performers on his podcast, The Tim Ferriss show.

KEY TAKEAWAYS OR BEST TIPS

- There is no formulaic path to health, wealth or wisdom.
- One of the first things you should learn to combat is peer pressure.
- Master the art of asking.
- Lean in to your fear.
- Meditate like a Guru.
- Start your day right.
- Choose depth over breadth.
- Escape the "busy" mentality.
- Just start. Boldness is the nucleus of achievement.
- Express your authentic self.
- You can only be creative if you make the time/space to be creative.

SUCCESS ANALYSIS – TOOLS OF TITANS

Your morning habits generally determine the course and success of your day, and thus, it is important to cultivagte and keep a routine that sparks your creativity and productivity.

Actor Jamie Foxx said his confidence comes from knowing that there's "nothing" on the other side of fear. "People are nervous for no reason," he explained. "When we talk about fear…it's in your head" (pg. 606).

MORE INFO			
Other books			

BOOK TITLE	The Millionaire Next Door: The Surprising Secrets
AUTHOR	Thomas J. Stanley
PUBLISHED	Taylor Trade Publishing, 1996

BEST QUOTES OR INSIGHTS

"Whatever your income, always live below your means"

"I am not impressed with what people own. But I'm impressed with what they achieve. I'm proud to be a physician. Always strive to be the best in your field.... Don't chase money. If you are the best in your field, money will find you."

"Good health, longevity, happiness, a loving family, self-reliance, fine friends ... if you [have] five, you're a rich man...."

"Wealth is more often the result of a lifestyle of hard work, perseverance, planning, and, most of all, self-discipline."

SUMMARY THEME OF BOOK

The book, Millionaire Next Door, shows us that simple spending and saving habits can lead to more money in the bank than most people earn in their life. The book also details how to avoid critical mistakes on your way to financial independence. The main points of the book include the ideals for maintain a practice of spending less than one individual can earn, developing a habit of avoiding buying's status symbols which are of no use.

KEY TAKEAWAYS OR BEST TIPS

"Many people who live in expensive homes and drive luxury cars do not actually have much wealth. Then, we discovered something even odder: Many people who have a great deal of wealth do not even live in upscale neighborhoods."

SUCCESS ANALYSIS – MILLIONAIRE NEXT DOOR

It develops an ideal that money is not a renewable resource, thus wise spending is essential.

The household must have similar values. A core theme in Stanley's book is that the family functions as a group with members having responsibilities in various areas: earning, spending, investing and maintenance.

MORE INFO	https://www.themillionairenextdoor.com/		
Other books			

BOOK TITLE	Trump 101: The Way to Success
AUTHOR	Donald J. Trump
PUBLISHED	Wiley (2006)

BEST QUOTES OR INSIGHTS

- "I have a billion dollars"
- "It has not been easy for me"
- "Beauty and elegance, whether in a woman, a building, or a work of art, is not just superficial or something pretty to see."

SUMMARY THEME OF BOOK

The book is split between twenty different factors which discusses inspirational genres. The book advices individuals to strive more in order to develop themselves and become greater successes. The book also inspires the readers to recognize the right business opportunities when they arrive. In Trump 101, Trump becomes personal mentor and coach as he shares tips, tactics, and strategies, which are designed to help you make the most of yourself, your career, and your life.

KEY TAKEAWAYS OR BEST TIPS

Frequently, the risk will be well worth the gamble, but sometimes it will be more than you can afford".

SUCCESS ANALYSIS – TRUMP 101

Here are some chapter names which reveal the secrets included:
- Don't Waste Your Life On Work You Don't Love: Passion Will Help You Do Better.
- Without Knowledge, You Don't Stand a Chance: Gain and Use Information to Your Advantage.
- Your Gut Is Your Best Advisor: Listen to Your Instincts.
- Surround Yourself with beauty: Enhance Every Aspect of Your Life.
- See the Whole Picture: Put Be Prepared for the Picture to Change.

MORE INFO			
Other books			

BOOK TITLE	Limitless: Upgrade Your Brain, Learn Anything Faster, and Unlock Your Exceptional Life Hardcover
AUTHOR	Jim Kwik (Author)
PUBLISHED	Hay House UK limited (2020)

BEST QUOTES OR INSIGHTS

"A light switch flipped on for me. Everyone should know this powerful information! My life's mission was born: to teach people the mindset, motivation, and methods that could move them from feeling disempowered to limitless."

"'Life is the C Between B and D.' The C standing for CHOICE with the B being birth and D for death"

SUMMARY THEME OF BOOK

Jim Kwik is one of th4e world's top brain coaches and written a manual for mental expansion and brain fitness. Limitless gives readers the ability to achieve more productivity, more transformation, more success and business achievement. Students can acheive this by changing their Mindset, Motivation, and Methods and through other skills, practices, exercises, and diet.

KEY TAKEAWAYS OR BEST TIPS

MY BIGGEST DREAMS WERE REALIZED

SUCCESS ANALYSIS - LIMITLESS			
The book contains effective ideals which have a high stance of "3M's" with the practical application in the book. Thus, the book describes that unlocking the developmental powers which targets the metacognition in an individual is effective for an effective development of the team and company.			
MORE INFO			
Other books			

Appendix – The Leadership and Consciousness Grid by Mentz

This is an experimental grid based on project management leadership principles which seeks to align the tasks of the: individual with the team and then find a congruent aspect of consciousness.

Mission Steps	Analysis	Consciousness
Problem	Understanding the Problem	Your Purpose
Analysis – Analyze Situation/Goal	Organize Correct Data	Your Beliefs about Data
Intel - Cultivate data and inputs to create the Mission and its needs.	Analyze tools and computation.	Your Skills that are built in.
Diagnosis - Diagnose problem and solutions.	What Information do you need to be successful.	Your Mindset and ability to Analyze
Planning - Develop a plan using experts	What is the situation and can it be fixed?	Your Synergy with the Team
Diagram or Chart the Mission into Phases	What is needed to fix or eliminate the problem.	Your Comprehension of the Mission
Human Performance - Engage Team Selection via tactical HR Human Resources.	Using assets to help team maximize performance	Seek to uncover assets not on resume. Mind, body, soul, culture.
Assets - Leaders and team must be equipped, skilled, and have access to quality information, tools, and data assets.	Selection of Human and Non Human Assets.	What management style are you most comfortable using? For you and your Teams?
Execute-ability - Determine methods of execution of the plan or mission	Methodologies are subjective.	What is collateral win or acceptable loss.
Comprehension Factor - Ability to understand and articulate the plan	Skill sets. Understanding the Game and Rules of Engagement	Processes of learning or retaining information.
Task Management - Prioritize the plans tasks in subsets or increments.	Isolating which skills and equipment is most efficient and effective.	What systems are you most comfortable using to monitor and implement tasks.
Contingency Planning	Clearly understanding contingency measures and how to execute them.	As an individual, learning the best process or steps for contingencies.

Landscape and Typography of the Mission	Understanding Culture, Terrain, Typography or the field and weather conditions.	How will you navigate as a unit or team? What tools or systems will you use.
External Systems used in Battle	Execution. When, What, How, When, Where and Why.	Mental faculties and skill to best use systems in any place on earth. Language, Typography, Laws etc.
Internal Systems used in Battle	Protecting Data, Communications, and Need to Know.	Individual proficiency in using systems amongst the team.
Communications - Mandate and itemize communication channels and methods.	Communications systems, Backups, Disaster Recovery Systems, Systems to account for all team members.	Mentally understand dialects, terminology, and languages.
TimeFrame - Create timeframe to Execute or deadlines for each task which coordinate with the rest of the team roles.	Incrementalization of the tasks, goals and time frame of the execution of the mission plan.	Individual fitness of each team member. Backup team members to replace anyone before or during mission.
Sustainability of the team vision, mission and roles.	What else is needed to make this team whole.	Do we have the energy, tools and knowhow to succeed.
Continuous Education - Education of team is continuous until mission date.	Methods of learning, experiential, online, group etc.	Individual skills, education, competencies. Conscientious skills.
Culture - Create a culture of extreme excellence based on stats, results and accuracy of each role.	Constructing a culture. What is the essence of the culture. Why is it needed?	Culture, Consciousness and Conscience are all vital.
No Assumptions - Incomplete data areas must be filled and sought to be filled incessantly.	Continuous analysis and seeking accurate data.	Mentally understand how any change in data affects mission and contingencies.
Synergistic - Team excellence, synergy, trust and group dynamics.	What are the ways to create trust, bonding, and synergy?	Belief in each other.
Response-Ability - Ownership of results and the mindset of success.	Collecting and analyzing data, stats to scientifically understand results.	

Unit Consciousness - Healthy body, mind, soul and Ego in tandem with the team. Team achievement consciousness.	Documenting balance of each.	Team is units, units have professionalism and style. Utilize both methods and style for best results.
Efficiencies - Simplifying tasks and roles for efficiency with are customized for any goals or mission.	Measuring efficiencies to maximize results and reduce or eliminate errors.	Removing fear of making errors and cultivating success and performance.
Hazards and Perils - Risk analysis is essential to be prepared for anticipated risk and ways to overcome such risk.	What types of hazards and perils are common for this specific mission.	Which assets best fit the success, risk and contingencies of this objective.
Enemy or Competitive Environment – Who can hurt you and how? Does the enemy need to be avoided, confronted, or eliminated?	Creating dossiers and research for study by team members so that all understand the nature of the adversary.	How do you get past your preconceptions of the opponent and cultivate a realistic knowledge and view of the adversary.
Decentralized – Roles spread out with each team member having backup skills to compensate for any weakness created by the accident, elements or enemy.	How do you select or appoint the most qualified backup and contingency assets, people and objectives.	Creating a responsiveness and quick/effective change of authority to maximize leadership
Individuation - Goals with designated roles.	How the objective and role of the individual changes in the course of the mission.	The mindset needed for each role. i.e weather, language, skills.
What is the Total Purpose of the Mission – Defined objectives. What is the Target of the Objective. Define Success	What is the optimum target and chief goal of the Mission making sure the team clearly understands this.	Creating a consciousness of success where all key players comprehend the essence and tasks needed to be successful
Authorizations - Delegated authority and Backup authority	How to document authority.	Parameters of Authority
Confidence Factor - Belief in achievement potentiality of mission-goal by leader and team.	Knowing the pros and cons of the Mission or Adversary.	Using individual and team assets to win.

SWOT analysis of each role and overall goal.		
Implementation – How to implement each task by each role member to complete of finish the objective successfully.	Visualizing and understanding the plans steps to complete each taxk.	Being Contemplative in Action. Staying aware and connected.
Calculated Execution - Quick and calculated decisions ready to utilize.	Understanding the implementation but assessing and adapting course continuously.	Using the power or praxis and power of now to respond in a mindful way and warriors speed.
Monitor Results – Continuous Information and Data Extraction CIDE	Knowing what to monitor. Having the right tools to monitor.	Cause and Effect are related. Every bit of data or action, or omission creates assumptions & consequences.
Continuous Improvement - Continually improve team roles, skills, and education while learning from data.	Ability to analyze data and activities to see what works and what does not.	Using awareness and right action to continuously adapt and innovate abilities.
Incentives - Systems of incentives and motivation.	Acknowledge success and excellence. Reward excellence and results with words, accolades, awards, and incentives.	
Documentation and Harvest of Data.	Accurate sources creates proper historical information.	Righteous understanding and comprehension creates the most powerful weapon which is wisdom.

Author Biography – George Mentz, Esq.

Commissioner George Mentz JD MBA CILS is a global entrepreneur trained in international law who has worked or traveled in over 40 nations worldwide. Mentz is an international award winning author and educator based in the United States. Mentz is the first business and law professor in the USA to be multi credentialed in: international law, management consulting, wealth management/financial consulting, and financial planning along with having an earned MBA and JD/Doctor of Jurisprudence degree and US law license.

Counselor Mentz is one of the few JD/MBA holders in the USA to earn a CILS Graduate Cert./Diploma in International Legal Studies. Mentz is the Titular Seigneur of the Feif of Blondel in Guernsey which is a legally registered Fief that is over 700 years old. Mentz is a US Commissioner for the White House Presidential Scholars Program in the USA. Mentz received his DSS Doctor of Spiritual Studies from the Emerson Institute and is a Member of the ANTN Affiliated New Thought Network. Mentz established the Global Association for the Chartered Economist ® and educational programs in the USA, EU and Africa that are offered worldwide.

This is a first of its kind primer on economic and business philosophy. The book discusses many of the great gurus of economics and finance. The manuscript contains much historical information in international business and economic policy. The book has key information top themes and ideas of the greatest philosophers in economics and business over the centuries up till the present day along with the basics of the US Economic System.

www.gmentz.com

www.ingramcontent.com/pod-product-compliance
Lightning Source LLC
Chambersburg PA
CBHW070851220526
45466CB00005B/1959